Hair, There, and Everywhere

A Book About Growing Up

First edition for the United States,
its territories and dependencies and
Canada published in 2008 by
Barron's Educational Series, Inc.

First published in 2008
by Franklin Watts
Hachette Children's Books
338 Euston Road
London, NW1 3BH

Text & design © Two's Company
2008
Illustrations © Sarah Naylor

All inquiries should be addressed to:
Barron's Educational Series, Inc.
250 Wireless Blvd.
Hauppauge, NY 11788
www.barronseduc.com

ISBN-13: 978-0-7641-3904-8
ISBN-10: 0-7641-3904-5

Library of Congress Catalog
   No.: 2007937777

Printed and bound in China
9 8 7 6 5 4 3 2 1

Hair, There, and Everywhere

A Book About
Growing Up

By Jacqui Bailey

BARRON'S

Contents

Your amazing body

You have the most amazing body.

Think of all the things you can do with it. You can run and jump, bend and twist, lift things up and throw them through the air. You can see and hear, touch and feel, taste, smell, shout, and sing.

Our bodies are all made in much the same way, no matter what size, shape, or even sex we are.

What's even more amazing is the fact that your body built itself. With some help from your mom and dad, it built your skin, bones, blood and muscles, your ears, eyes, eyelashes, and toenails. It made you a heart to pump your blood around your body, lungs to breathe in air, and a brain to tell them all what to do.

Self-made

By the time you were born your body had everything it needed, but it didn't stop there. It kept on growing and changing every part of you. And guess what? Your body will keep on doing this all through your life, often without you realizing it.

This book is all about you and your body. It explains how you were born and how you changed from a baby to a child. Most of all, this book tells you about what your body is going to do next. You and your body are about to go on a great adventure …

… it's called growing up.

Cells R Us

Your entire body is built out of millions of tiny cells. Most are so small they can only be seen with a microscope.

These cells are always wearing out, but your body makes new ones to replace them all through your life.

The different parts of your body are made from different types of cells.

red blood cells make your blood

muscle cells make your muscles

I'm a bundle of nerves!

nerve cells carry messages between your brain and the rest of your body

How did I begin?

You began as just two separate cells

— an egg cell and a sperm cell. The egg cell was inside your mom and the sperm cell was inside your dad. When your mom's egg cell and your dad's sperm cell joined together they made a completely new cell — YOU!

Inside your mom

Your mom has lots of tiny egg cells inside her body. They are stored in two little walnut-shaped sacks called ovaries, down low in her belly. Every month, one egg leaves one ovary and travels along a tube to a part of your mom's body called the womb or uterus. If the egg cell doesn't join up with a sperm cell along the way, it moves to the bottom of the uterus and into another short, stretchy tube called the vagina. Then the egg leaves the vagina through an opening between your mom's legs.

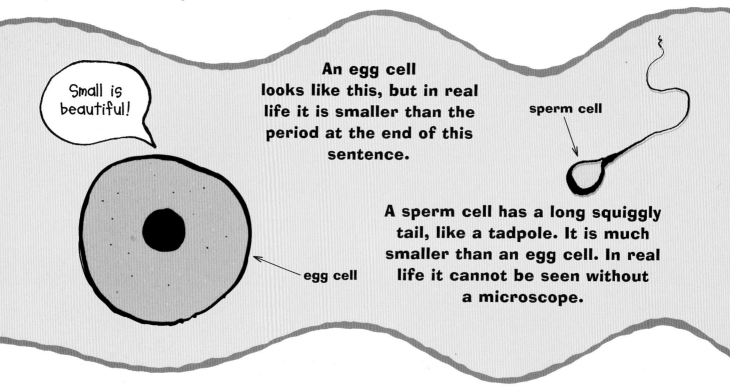

Small is beautiful!

An egg cell looks like this, but in real life it is smaller than the period at the end of this sentence.

egg cell

sperm cell

A sperm cell has a long squiggly tail, like a tadpole. It is much smaller than an egg cell. In real life it cannot be seen without a microscope.

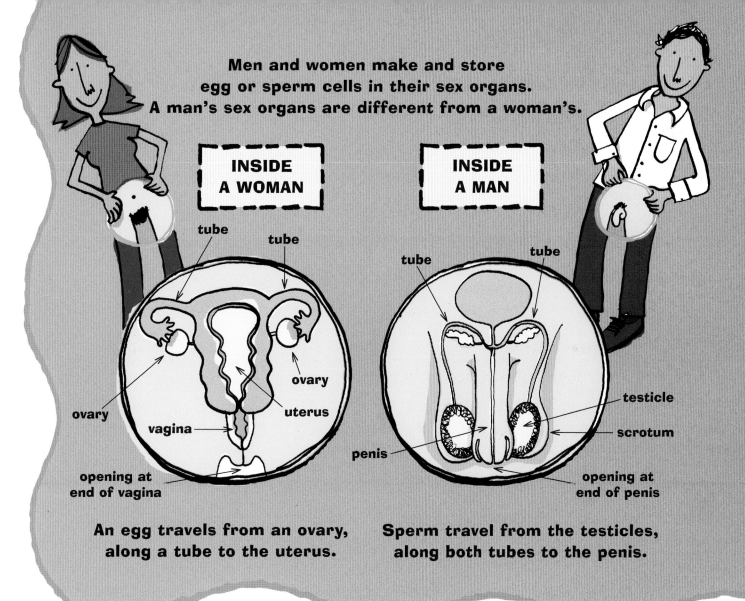

Men and women make and store egg or sperm cells in their sex organs. A man's sex organs are different from a woman's.

INSIDE A WOMAN

INSIDE A MAN

tube — tube

tube — tube

ovary

ovary — uterus

vagina

opening at end of vagina

testicle

scrotum

penis

opening at end of penis

An egg travels from an ovary, along a tube to the uterus.

Sperm travel from the testicles, along both tubes to the penis.

Inside your dad

Your dad makes millions and millions of sperm cells every day. He makes them inside two plum-shaped bags called testicles. The testicles are carried in a loose, wrinkly sack of skin called the scrotum, which hangs just behind the penis. Sperm cells are stored in the testicles for a few weeks. If the cells aren't used they dissolve to make room for new ones.

To make you, your dad's sperm cell had to get inside your mom. The way your mom and dad did this was by having intercourse. This is also called "making love," or "having sex." Moms and dads have intercourse when they love each other and when they want to make a baby.

One in a Million!

When a man and a woman have intercourse they hold each other very close and the man puts his penis inside the woman's vagina. Eventually, the man's sperm cells shoot out of the opening at the end of his penis into the woman's vagina. The sperm cells swim along the vagina and into the uterus. They are all searching for the egg cell and it's a race against time.

1. The sperm cells race toward the egg.

Me first!

2. When the sperm find the egg they try to get inside it.

3. One sperm gets inside. The egg is now fertilized.

The race begins

The man sends about 400 million sperm into the woman's vagina, but only one of them can join up with the egg. Most of them don't even reach the tubes at the top of the uterus. Of those that do, some go into one tube and some into the other — but only one tube has an egg in it.

Finding the egg

Only a few hundred sperm actually reach the egg. They wiggle around it, trying desperately to get inside. If one sperm manages to push its way in, the egg instantly makes a barrier to keep the others out. The winning sperm's squiggly tail drops off and the two cells join up and become one new cell — a fertilized egg cell.

Soon there will be millions of us.

Burp!

4. The fertilized cell divides into two cells, then four, then eight, and on and on.

5. After 8 weeks the bundle of cells has grown a head, eyes, arms, and legs.

The great divide
The new cell isn't just one cell for very long. It copies itself and divides into two cells. Then the two cells divide into four, the four divide into eight — and so on. The dividing cells clump together into a bundle. As more cells are added, the bundle gradually gets bigger and moves out of the tube and into the uterus.

A bigger bundle
The bundle stays in the uterus, slowly making more and more cells. After about eight weeks the bundle is still less than 1 inch (3 cm) long, but now it is made of millions of cells. It also has a head, eyes, arms, and legs ...

... it is you!

How did I grow?

When you were born you were almost as big as a football. You had been in your mom's uterus for about 38 weeks, and in that time you doubled and doubled in size. In fact, you grew more quickly than you ever will at any other time in your life.

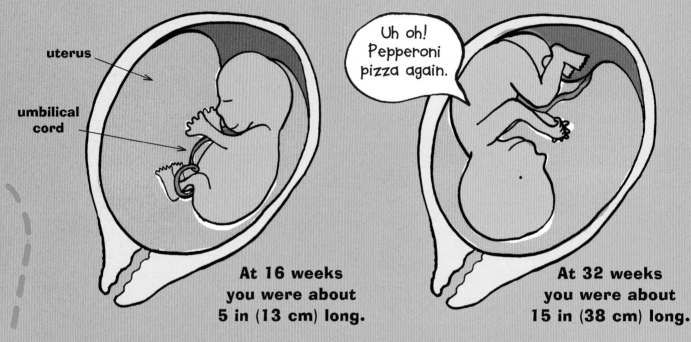

uterus

umbilical cord

Uh oh! Pepperoni pizza again.

At 16 weeks you were about 5 in (13 cm) long.

At 32 weeks you were about 15 in (38 cm) long.

On the inside

While you were inside your mom's uterus you floated in a bag full of liquid called the placenta. The liquid protected you from bumps and knocks as your mom moved around.

You did not need to eat, drink, or breathe for yourself inside the uterus. All your food, drink, and oxygen from the air came to you through a soft, bendy tube called the umbilical cord. The umbilical cord reached from the wall of your mom's uterus to your tummy. Everything your mom ate or drank, you ate and drank, too.

You could move around inside the uterus. You could see light coming through your mom's skin and hear her stomach rumbling and her heart beating. You heard noises from outside, as well.

Between 38 and 42 weeks you were about 20 in (50 cm) long, and you were ready to be born.

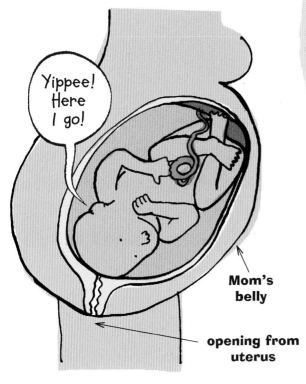

Yippee! Here I go!

Mom's belly

opening from uterus

Other birth ways

Not all babies are born the same way. Some come out feet first. This is called a breech birth and a doctor usually helps the baby to come out.

Sometimes a doctor carefully cuts an opening into the side of the mother's uterus and lifts the baby out. Then the cut is sewn up. This is called a cesarean birth (because Julius Caesar is thought to have been born this way). The mother is given painkillers so she does not feel the operation.

Coming down!

Being born

As you got bigger you took up more and more space inside your mom's belly, and it got bigger too. When you were ready to be born you probably turned upside down, so your head pressed on the stretchy opening at the bottom of her uterus.

After a lot of pushing and squeezing by your mom, you were most likely born head first from the opening between your mom's legs. As soon as you were born you opened your mouth and started to breathe. You

may have yelled a little, too. Then the nurse or doctor cut the umbilical cord to separate you from your mom, and you were given to your parents for your first hug ever.

Getting bigger

You were pretty small when you were born, but you didn't stay that way for long. By the time you were two years old you were already about half as tall as you will be when you are an adult.

Walking and talking

Our bodies kept on growing from the moment we were born all through our childhood. And the bigger our body gets, the more we can do with it.

A newborn baby can't do very much for itself, not even sit up. But babies soon grow stronger. By the time you were seven months old you could probably sit upright. At about ten months you were crawling around, and by 14 months you were probably standing up and walking.

Once you could walk there was no stopping you. When you were six you could run, jump, and climb. You had learned to talk, feed yourself, and play — and you were ready to go to school.

Changing shape

As you grew, you also changed your shape. Babies have short arms and legs and large

Gah bah goo?

Up! Up!

Can't catch me.

10 months

14 months

6 years

heads compared to the rest of their body. But as you grew taller your body lengthened and your arms and your legs got longer.

Speeding up
Between the ages of about ten and 13, the speed at which you grow increases and your height seems to shoot up. At 13 you will be a teenager and you will keep on growing for most of your teens. Then you will stop. You will have reached the right height for your body and you will not get any taller. As far as your body is concerned you will be ...

... a grown up.

I'm growing fast.

I think I've stopped.

10-13 years

19 years

How tall?

How tall you are as an adult depends mostly on how tall your parents are. If your parents are short, medium, or tall, then you probably will be too.

But other things can affect your height as well, such as the food you eat. If you eat a mixture of foods each day that includes plenty of fruit and vegetables, a few portions of meat, fish, cheese, eggs or beans, and some bread, rice or pasta, then you will probably grow to your full size.

If you do not have enough of these things then you might not grow as tall as you could.

Turning into a teen

Becoming a teenager is a strange and special time. Your body is changing in all sorts of ways, and not just on the outside. Welcome to the wonderful world of PUBERTY!

The word "puberty" is a more scientific way of saying "growing up." But it doesn't only mean getting taller. It means that your body is changing from a child into an adult. In particular, it means becoming able to reproduce — to make babies.

Don't panic!

Being able to make babies is not the same thing as actually making them. You've got a long way to go before you need to worry about that. In the first place, you have to be able to produce egg or sperm cells — remember pages 8 and 9? And to do that, you need to have mature (another way of saying "grown up")

You could be the first of your friends to begin puberty, or the last. Either way it makes no difference. There is no good or bad time to start — just the right time for you!

sex organs. So puberty is not so much about how YOU grow up, but how your SEX ORGANS grow up!

Ups and downs

Of course, while your sex organs are growing up, many other changes happen to you as well — to your

Have you started puberty yet?

Oh, yeah. Ages ago.

Dunno.

body and to the way you think and feel about things. This is why puberty is such a confusing time. It is an in-between time when you are no longer a child, but you haven't yet learned to be an adult. You are finding out all sorts of new things about yourself and the world, and sometimes this is fun and exciting, and at other times it is a little scary and confusing.

The important thing to remember is that you are not alone. Everyone in the world goes through the same ups and downs that puberty brings — even your parents, or the grumpy neighbor across the street!

When will I start?

We all go through puberty, but exactly how and when it happens is different for each of us.

Girls usually start puberty before boys — often around the ages of 10 or 11, but it might be a year or two earlier, or a few years later.

Boys usually begin between the ages of 11 and 13 but, again, it might be earlier or later than this.

Try asking your mom or dad what age they were. The odds are that you will start puberty at roughly the same age they did.

What makes puberty start?

It's all because of hormones. Hormones are a special group of chemicals that your body makes inside you. Your body makes lots of different types of hormones and they all work on different parts of you. But basically they work as messengers — they tell a part of your body to either start doing something, or stop doing something.

Sending messages

Your body is sending itself hormone messages all the time — making sure that everything is working properly and doing what has to be done. There are thousands and thousands of them darting around inside you.

Hormones tell your body when to start growing and when to stop — and even in what order different parts of you should grow. They control how energetic you feel, or how tired and sleepy, how hot or cold your body gets, and how much you sweat.

They can make your heart beat faster and they can make you feel angry or moody. There are even hormones that tell other hormones what to do. And, of course, there are hormones that tell your body when to start puberty.

It's all in your head

It's true — puberty begins in your brain! One part of your brain sends a hormone message to another part of your brain telling it to start making two particular types of hormone. These two types of hormone act like an alarm clock on your sex organs, telling them to wake up and start doing what they are supposed to do.

Ready ... set ... go!

If you are a boy, the hormones wake up your testicles and tell them to get ready to make sperm. If you are a girl, the hormones go to your ovaries and tell them to get ready to send out eggs. They also tell sex organs to start making hormones of their own. And it's these hormones, the ones made in your sex organs, that set off all sorts of other changes that happen to you during puberty ...

Carried along

Your body has about 3 liters of blood in it. When you are full grown you will have more, maybe 5 or 6 liters.

Blood travels around and around your body inside thousands of tubes called blood vessels. Blood vessels are spread throughout your body so that the blood can get to every cell.

... phew!

Blood is your body's delivery system. It carries vital supplies to your cells, including food and oxygen for energy, white blood cells to fight off germs — and your hormones!

All change

One minute your clothes fit you and you barely think about your body from one day to another. The next, it seems as if all your clothes are too small and your body belongs to someone else! That's puberty.

Puberty makes you and your body feel awkward and uncomfortable. Suddenly, your hair won't go right, your feet are too big, you keep bumping into things, and you wish your ears didn't stick out so much.

Help! My clothes have shrunk!

your jeans suddenly feel too short and your sleeves seem to stop at your elbows. Your hands and feet get bigger too, and, until you get used to their new size, you feel as if you are always falling over things. But don't worry, the rest of your body soon catches up.

Growth spurts

There are times when you suddenly grow very quickly. These are known as growth spurts and they happen over a period of about three to six years.

Your arms and legs get longer first, which is why

Sooner or later

Before puberty, boys and girls grow in much the same way, with boys growing just a little bit faster. During puberty all this changes. Girls usually start their growth spurts about two

years earlier than boys. This is why, in any group of 12-year-olds, the girls often tower over the boys.

But when boys do get their growth spurts, they usually go on growing for longer than girls. They also tend to grow more quickly, which is why many men end up taller than women. However, as everyone is different from everyone else, there are also short men and tall women.

Girls reach their full height at about 16 or 17. Boys often keep growing until they are 19 or even 20.

In your sleep

The hormone that controls your growth works mostly at night while you are asleep. If your sleep is disturbed, or you go to bed late, less growth hormone is released.

Children who regularly do not get enough sleep often do not grow as much as they could. Which means, I'm afraid, that your mom is right — you really do need your sleep!

Upwards and outwards

At the same time that you are getting taller you are also getting heavier and the shape of your body is changing.

Bones and muscles

Boys' bones and muscles get longer, stronger, and more bulky. Their chest gets wider and their shoulders broader. More muscle and heavier bones add up to more weight.

How big your muscles are is different for everyone. Some boys worry about the size of their muscles, but it is best to let your muscles grow naturally, rather than lifting weights to make them bigger, as you could end up injuring them instead.

Chest fat

Sometimes boys get a swelling behind the nipples on their chest that may also feel a bit sore. If this happens to you it DOES NOT mean that you are turning into a woman and growing breasts! It is perfectly normal for your body to put some fat on your chest even if it doesn't happen to everyone — so don't let it bother you. It will sort itself out in a year or so, but if you are really worried about it, talk to your parents and your doctor.

I have a naturally slimmer build!

Remember that everyone is different. Some boys have slim bodies and others are more muscular.

Eating healthy food and getting lots of exercise is the best way to keep your body in shape during puberty. See pages 68–72.

Hips and curves

Girls get broader in the hips during puberty and their shape often becomes softer and curvier. Their breasts start to swell (see pages 32–33) and they put on weight. Partly the weight is due to bigger bones and muscles, and partly it is due to an increase in body fat. Girls put on more body fat than boys during puberty.

Baby fat

Some girls worry about putting on weight, but at this point in your life your body is doing just what it needs to do. Girls need the extra body fat to help prepare their bodies for having babies some day. It is a bad idea to try and stop your body from putting on this extra weight by dieting or not eating properly. You could make yourself ill and prevent your body from growing normally.

Again, how much weight you will put on varies from person to person. If you are worried about it, talk to someone who will give you good advice about what is a healthy weight for you, such as your parents, school nurse, or your doctor.

How do I look?

There aren't many people who go through puberty without worrying about how they look to the rest of the world. At some point or another, we all become incredibly self-conscious.

Being self-conscious makes us worry about the ways in which our bodies do or don't change, and whether or not we will get teased about it. For example, it might seem to you as if everyone in your class is getting taller when you haven't grown so much as an extra hair! Or that all the other girls you know are developing breasts and buying bras when you aren't. Or you might look at people in magazines or TV shows and think that your body will never be as ... muscular ... slim ... curvy as theirs.

Sigh... wish my hair was like Beth's. She looks so pretty.

Hi Beth, are you going to Anna's party on Saturday?

Sigh... wish I was tall and slim like Alice.

I hope so, if my parents will let me.

All the same

The thing to remember is that we all feel that way sometimes — even the coolest, best-looking person you know. We all worry about whether other people like us and find us attractive, and most of all, whether we "fit in." But just as the shortest kid in the class worries about being short, so the tallest kid

Feeding frenzy

Like most teenagers, you may suddenly find yourself craving lots of rich foods during puberty. Yep! It is those hormones again! Because your body is growing, your hormones are making sure you get plenty to eat to feed that growth. Just try not to overdo it!

SCOFF! SCOFF!

feels self-conscious about being too tall. And while some girls worry about having small breasts, others worry that theirs are too big. In fact, there is no perfect figure or way of looking. We are all designed to look different, and we all find different people attractive in different ways.

Being teased

Just about everybody gets teased at some time or another, but that doesn't make it less hurtful when it happens to you. The trick is knowing that teasing can only get to you if you let yourself take someone's nasty remark seriously. If you laugh at it, or just shrug and walk away, the person who said it is left looking bad, not you! Try to remember that people who tease others often do it because they feel unhappy about themselves and are trying to cover it up by making someone else feel bad.

Like yourself

Lots of the differences that we worry about during puberty disappear as we get older. In the meantime, keep in mind that differences are good and try to accept your body the way that it is, especially over the next few years, while it plays all sorts of tricks on you …

… read on!

More body stuff

So, you get taller and heavier and your shape changes — is that it? No way, that's just the easy stuff. Then there's the hair, the sweaty skin, the voice ... not to mention the pimples!

Hair there ...

One day you notice the hairs on your arms and legs are getting darker and thicker. But it doesn't stop there. Hair starts appearing around your penis and testicles if you are a boy, and around your vagina if you are a girl.

This is called pubic hair and it is usually darker and curlier than the rest of your body hair. Over the next few years the patch of pubic hair will grow thicker, and you might also have a line of darker hair leading from your pubic hair to your navel.

... and everywhere

Patches of hair will also appear under your armpits, and boys often grow hair on their chest. Girls may have a few dark hairs growing around their nipples as well.

Then there's the hair on your face. Boys grow darker hair on their upper lip first, then over the chin and cheeks and down their neck. Girls may also have darker hairs on their upper lip. It's all perfectly normal.

Loving it, or losing it

Body hair is a strange thing. Some people think it's great, some people hate it, and lots of people don't think about it all. However you feel about it, it's best to just let it grow to begin with. Then, if you want to, you can start thinking about whether or not you want to remove some of it.

Boys and girls grow body hair in much the same places, the only difference is that some people are naturally more hairy than others.

Shaving

Maybe I'll grow a beard...

Boys often start shaving their face before they really need to. Get some advice from your dad or another older man first, but don't rush. Remember that, once you start, you could be doing it pretty much every day for the rest of your life.

Girls, talk to your mom or an older friend before you start shaving your legs or armpits. Shaving is quick and easy, but the hairs will grow back stronger and darker, and it can make your skin sore. NEVER shave your face (or anything other than your legs and armpits) — there are different ways of getting rid of facial and other hair if it really bothers you.

In a sweat

Along with all the other stuff that's going on in your body you find that you are sweating more than you used to and, now, your sweat is stinky!

Poring out

Your body sweats when it gets too hot. An overheated body isn't good for you so your brain sends out hormones telling your skin to sweat. During puberty there are many more hormones in your body than usual, and this means that you sweat more.

Your skin has lots of tiny holes in it called pores (see page 30). Below the pores are little sacks called sweat glands. These make sweat and release it through your pores. When the sweat in your skin gets outside your body it evaporates — turns from a liquid to a gas — and floats away, taking some of your body heat with it, so you cool down.

In the mix

Sweat is mostly made of water and is not particularly stinky — until it mixes with the bacteria on your skin. Bacteria are tiny living things that cannot be seen without a microscope. There are millions of them all around us. Most are harmless, but when they mix with sweat, they make the sweat smell.

Bacteria particularly like living in warm, damp places, such as your armpits, feet, and sex organs.

It's not me, it's my bacteria!

Do not despair

Luckily there is an amazing cure for stinky sweat — it's called washing! Wash your whole body once a day, and pay special attention to those warm, damp areas. Change your clothes regularly, too. If you want to wear the same clothes more than once, use your nose to tell you if yesterday's sweat is hanging around on them.

Clean clothes and washing every day should do it, but if you are really worried about your body smell then you could also use a deodorant or an anti-perspirant. Don't use them instead of washing, though, and don't use them on your sex organs as you could get a rash.

Voice control

When you talk, shout, or sing the sounds come from a part of your throat called the voice box or larynx.

Everyone's larynx gets bigger during puberty and everyone's voice gets a little deeper. But a boy's larynx grows more than a girl's. This is why older boys have a bulge in the front of their throat called an Adam's Apple. It is really a grown-up larynx.

While their larynx is growing most boys find their voice slides around all over the place without their control, from gruff to squeaky and back again. In other words, their voice is "breaking." It can be a little embarrassing, but don't worry, it won't last forever.

Spot the spot

Just when you think you've got the whole hairy, sweaty, smelly thing sorted out, you look in the mirror one morning and scream — pimples!

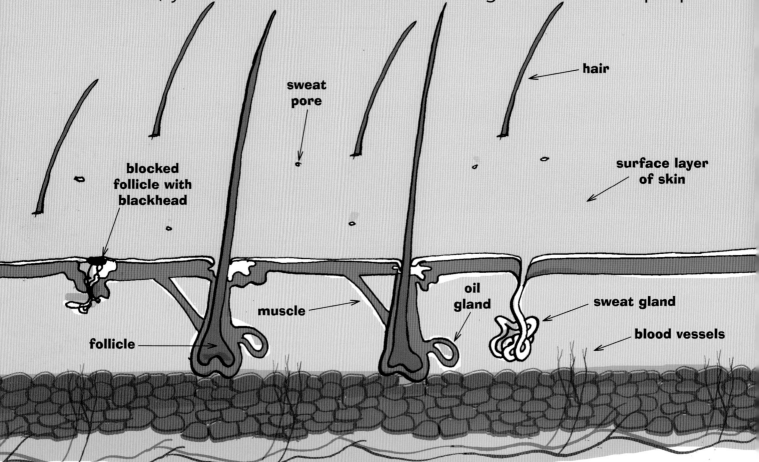

hair

sweat pore

surface layer of skin

blocked follicle with blackhead

muscle

oil gland

sweat gland

blood vessels

follicle

Covered in oil

In addition to sweat glands, your skin contains oil glands, too. Every hair on your body grows from a root in your skin called a follicle. Each follicle has its own oil gland. The oil keeps the hair healthy and shiny, but during puberty your oil glands go into overdrive and produce lots of extra oil, making your skin and hair feel very greasy.

This is what your skin looks like under the surface.

If too much oil builds up around a follicle or a pore it can get blocked. If the block forms under the skin it makes a whitehead — a small lump with a white spot in the center. If it forms on the skin's surface it makes a blackhead — a small black dot. If bacteria from your skin get into the blocked follicle it can get infected. The spot swells up into a red throbbing lump with a yellow center that feels like a volcano on your face.

What is acne?

Acne is just another way of saying you've got pimples. It usually means you have a number of pimples that keep appearing. Acne can break out on your neck, upper body, and on your face.

Some people think acne is caused by not washing enough or by eating too many greasy or sweet foods, but this is not true. Acne is caused by hormones making your skin produce too much oil.

Keeping it clear

So what can you do about it? Well, it helps if you keep your skin and hair clean. Regular washing stops the oil from building up. Use warm water and a gentle soap, but don't scrub your skin. Don't over wash it either, as your skin will get dry and crack.

Keep your hands away from your pimples and don't squeeze them. If you must touch them, wash your hands first. This helps keep bacteria away. Boys and girls should both use a non-oily moisturizer to protect their skin, get plenty of sleep, and drink LOTS of water. Sounds boring, I know, but it works. Finally, if your pimples make you really miserable, see a doctor. Now, back to those ...

... sex organs!

Guess what? Chocolate and fries have nothing to do with causing pimples or acne.

It's still not good for you to eat too much of them, though.

Girls only

Some of the changes that happen during puberty will happen to you only if you are a girl. In fact, these are the changes that put you firmly in the girl camp. Celebrate them! They are part of who you are.

About breasts

Okay, so not every girl is thrilled about growing breasts. This may be because having breasts tells the world that you are becoming a woman, and you might not feel quite ready for that. Or because magazines and newspapers are always featuring breasts as if their size and shape are important, so they become one more thing to worry about!

The truth is, breasts are just another part of your body. They are there because, if you have a baby, they will produce the milk to feed your baby.

A mother's milk is good for her baby's health and growth. But the size and shape of her breasts make no difference to how much milk they produce.

Size and shape are only important because some people think they are. Although, to be honest, no one can agree on this, either. Some people think small breasts are great and others think large breasts are great.

First a quick meal, then my nap.

When will they grow?

Breasts start growing quite early in puberty. Some girls will see a small swelling under their nipples when they are about 8 years old, others may not see anything until they are 13. Often, the circle of skin around your nipples (the areola) gets bigger and darker, and your nipples get bigger, too.

Breasts grow slowly — sometimes right through puberty and into your early twenties. As they grow they might feel a bit tingly or achy every now and then, and one side might look larger than the other for a while. Don't worry, they will even out, more or less, in the end, although no two breasts are ever exactly the same.

What about a bra?

There is no right or wrong time to start wearing a bra. The best time is when you feel ready to wear one. At some point you will probably find it more comfortable (and comforting) to wear a bra, especially when you are playing sports or being active.

At first, finding a bra that fits you properly can be a bit complicated. Ask your mom, older sister, or an older female friend to help you, and make sure you try the bra on before you buy it.

Before you buy

Many department stores and specialty shops have trained assistants who are happy to measure you for your correct bra size and give you advice about the types of bras available. It's well worth doing, even if you feel a little embarrassed!

Having periods

The really major event that happens to girls during puberty is starting their periods. Even if you know everything there is to know about it, your first period is always a big deal when it happens to you.

Periods Start Here!

Uh oh, something's happening...

Why do periods happen?

You have periods because you have egg cells. Once a month, one egg cell leaves one of your ovaries and travels toward your uterus.

While the egg is on its way, the uterus gets ready for its arrival. It grows a thick, soft lining on its inner walls to hold and protect the egg while it grows into a baby. However, the egg will ONLY attach itself to the lining if it has already been fertilized by a sperm cell — see page 8 for the chapter called "How did I begin?"

Breaking up

If the egg hasn't been fertilized it starts to break up. The uterus no longer needs its nice new lining, so it breaks up too, and turns into a lumpy liquid made up of lining mixed with blood. The blood carries everything down to the vagina and out of the opening at the end — taking what's left of the egg with it. This flow of blood is a period.

When will they start?

As with everything else to do with puberty, periods can start anywhere between the ages of 8 or 9, to 15 or even 16. They don't usually begin until after your breasts and pubic hair have started to grow.

Some months before your first period you might notice a clear, milky, or creamy liquid coming from your vagina. It doesn't have any smell, but it will leave a small stain on your underpants. The liquid is called a vaginal discharge. It comes from the walls of your vagina and it is a sign that your sexual organs are going into action.

Monthly cycles

Every girl's period happens in its own way and its own time, and often varies from month to month. Generally, periods happen every 28 to 30 days. This is called the menstrual cycle. But some women have a shorter cycle than this, and for others it's longer.

To begin with, you might have your first period and then miss a month or two. Or, you could have two periods in the same month. This is perfectly normal. Periods follow nobody's rules but their own!

Period points

● It may look like a lot, but the amount of blood you lose during a period usually ranges from a couple of spoonfuls to a cupful.

● The name "period" is short for menstruation period. It is also called menstruating.

Periods can be a pain!

Lots of girls worry about what it will be like to have a period and some find the whole thought of periods a nightmare! But although they can be annoying and uncomfortable sometimes, they are a healthy and perfectly natural process. You'll be amazed how quickly you get used to them.

How long do they last?

A period can last for two days or more than a week. You might have a heavy period with quite a lot of blood, or a light one with only a little blood or even just a few smears. You might find that your breasts feel a bit swollen or tender a day or two before, and your skin might break out in pimples. You could also feel unusually grumpy, or sad and emotional, or just "out of sorts" — or you might not feel any of these things at all.

Lots of women get pains, or cramps, in their belly before or at the start of their period. The pains can vary from mildly uncomfortable to downright agony. They are usually caused by muscles in the walls of your uterus, squeezing and relaxing to push out the lining and the blood. Some girls get very little pain and some get a lot. If you get period cramps there are lots of things you can do to help ease them. Talk to your mom, the school nurse, or your family doctor.

Don't worry. You go and lie down and I'll call your mother.

If you get a painful period at school, don't be embarrassed to ask for help from the school nurse or a female teacher.

What to wear?

When you have a period you need to wear something to soak up the blood and stop it from staining your clothes.

sanitary pad

At first, the best things to use are sanitary pads. These are strips of padded material that go inside your underpants, between your legs. They usually have sticky tape on one side to hold them in place.

Pads are easy to use and no one will be able to tell that you are wearing one. But you cannot wear them to go swimming.

Older girls often wear tampons. These are like squashed-up pads that fit inside your vagina. They are completely invisible except for a short string that you use to pull them out, and you can swim while wearing them. But it can take some practice getting used to putting them in.

Both types need to be changed at least every few hours during the day. Otherwise bacteria builds up and can cause an infection. Wash your hands before and after, and wrap up used ones and put them in a wastebasket.

tampon

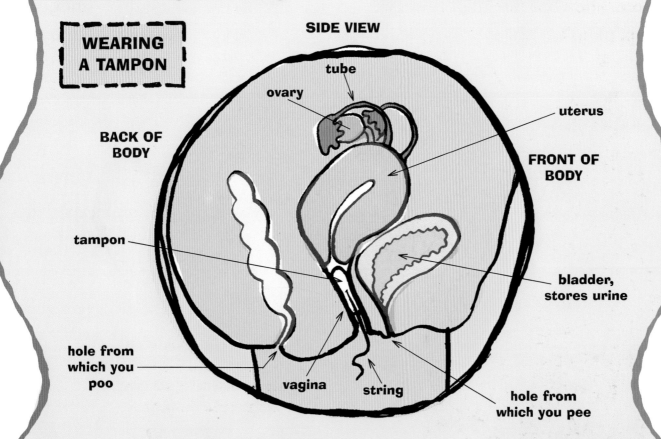

WEARING A TAMPON

SIDE VIEW

tube

ovary

uterus

BACK OF BODY

FRONT OF BODY

tampon

bladder, stores urine

hole from which you poo

vagina

string

hole from which you pee

You and your body

Starting your periods means that you need to be more aware of your body than you might have been before.

Be prepared

Try to get into the habit of noting the first day of your period in a diary or on a calendar. Then you can count forward to give yourself a rough idea of when your next period is due.

The first day of your period counts as Day 1, so if your periods are on a 28-day cycle, for example, your next period is due on Day 29 (give or take a day or two). It will take a while before your periods settle down into any kind of regular cycle, but you should eventually get some idea of how long your cycle is.

Getting to know you

It's a good idea to get to know your vulva, or outer sex organs, even if you feel embarrassed doing it.

Choose a comfortable place where you won't be disturbed. Lie or sit with your knees up, and hold a hand mirror between your legs. Sounds weird, I know, but it's a really useful thing to do. The diagram opposite will help you identify the correct parts.

How it feels

It is perfectly okay to feel your vulva. In fact, if you ever want to wear a tampon it's absolutely necessary to know where your vagina is and what it feels like inside. Many girls discover that touching their vulva feels pleasant and even exciting, especially if they rub the small bump at the front, called the clitoris. This is known as masturbating, and it is a completely safe and natural way to explore your body, so don't be ashamed of yourself if you do it too.

Taking care

You must keep your vulva clean, but don't try to clean inside your vagina — it cleans itself. Wash around the outside at least once a day with plain soap or body-wash and water. Make sure you wash and dry your vulva carefully, from front to back so that

you don't carry bacteria from your anus to your vagina and get an infection.

If your vagina ever gets sore or itchy, or you have a smelly discharge, you should see a doctor. Always look after your sex organs — they are an important part …

… of you.

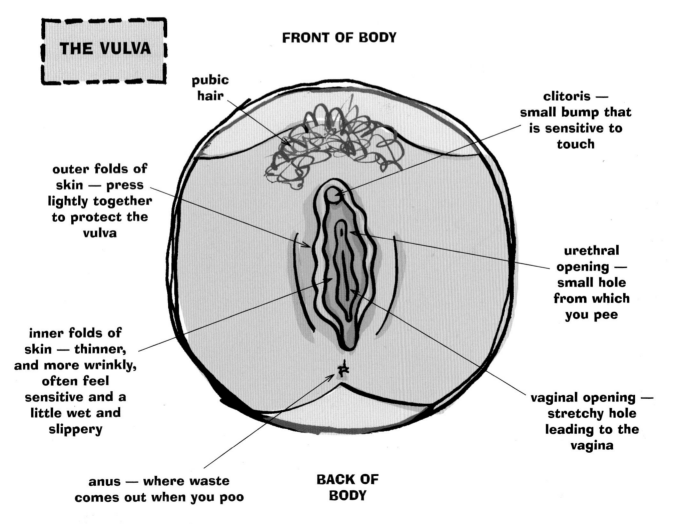

THE VULVA

FRONT OF BODY

pubic hair

clitoris — small bump that is sensitive to touch

outer folds of skin — press lightly together to protect the vulva

urethral opening — small hole from which you pee

inner folds of skin — thinner, and more wrinkly, often feel sensitive and a little wet and slippery

vaginal opening — stretchy hole leading to the vagina

anus — where waste comes out when you poo

BACK OF BODY

Boys only

Boys, too, get hit by hormones in ways that affect the parts of them that make them boys. Before puberty your testicles and penis are kind of small and don't do very much. Then they start to change …

The first thing that happens is that your testicles get bigger. Before puberty, testicles are roughly the size and shape of two grapes. Then hormones wake them up and they start to grow. When they reach their full size, each one will be about as big as a walnut in its shell.

> Testicles are also called nuts or balls.

The left testicle often hangs a bit lower than the right. This is so they don't bang into each other when you run around.

In the bag

Testicles hang outside the body in a skin bag called the scrotum. As the testicles grow, the scrotum gets bigger and baggier too. Sometimes white spots appear on it. These "spots" are where pubic hairs will grow, and are nothing to worry about.

Keeping cool

The reason your testicles hang outside your body is all to do with temperature. Testicles make and store millions of sperm every day, and sperm have to be kept at exactly the right temperature — not too hot and not too cold.

Tube journey

Each testicle is connected to a long thin tube called the epididymis, which is wrapped tightly around one

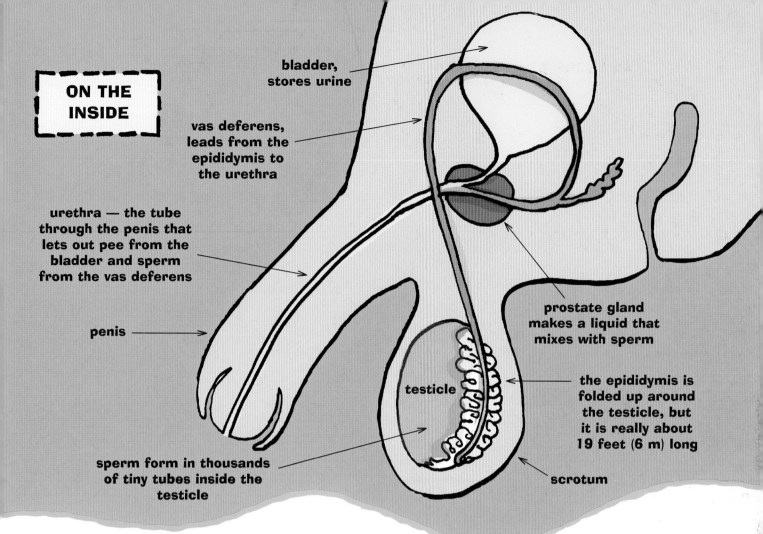

bladder, stores urine

vas deferens, leads from the epididymis to the urethra

urethra — the tube through the penis that lets out pee from the bladder and sperm from the vas deferens

penis

prostate gland makes a liquid that mixes with sperm

testicle

the epididymis is folded up around the testicle, but it is really about 19 feet (6 m) long

sperm form in thousands of tiny tubes inside the testicle

scrotum

side of the testicle. The epididymis leads to another tube called the vas deferens. This loops from the testicle around the bladder to your penis.

Sperm begin life in the testicles then move into the epididymis for 4 to 6 weeks, gradually working their way along the folded tube to the vas deferens. At this point, the sperm either dissolve and are absorbed back into the body — or they head off on a one-way trip toward the penis.

Safe and secure

Testicles are easily damaged. A kick or a hit, even a light one, can cause extreme pain — as you will know if it has ever happened to you — as well as bruising and swelling.

Be safe rather than sorry and always wear a protective "box" or "cup" when playing sports.

Measuring up

Some time after your testicles get bigger your penis starts getting longer and thicker. For most boys, penis size suddenly becomes a big issue.

Every one is different

At some point, every boy worries about the size of his penis. Exactly when and how quickly your penis and pubic hair grow is different for every boy, but believe me, everyone gets there in the end. And, in spite of what some people might say, there is no ideal length or shape for a penis — each one is individual, like its owner.

Penis at work

No matter what your penis looks like they all do the same things, and size and shape make no difference at all to how well they work. Your penis basically has two jobs, you pee out of it, and you release sperm from it — and no, you can't do both at the same time.

Releasing sperm from your penis is called ejaculating. When you ejaculate, sperm rushes from the epididymis into the vas deferens and then into the urethra. This is the tube that leads down your penis to the opening at the end.

Humph! Mine's not that big and he's shorter than me.

I have enough sperm to populate the world!

Sperm fluid

As it travels through the vas deferens, the sperm mixes with a fluid that helps carry it along. The fluid is called semen. When semen comes out of your penis it is slippery, white, and milky looking. Each ejaculation produces about a spoonful or so of semen, but each spoonful can have as many as 500 MILLION sperm in it!

However, before you can ejaculate you usually need to have an erection. This means that your penis goes hard and stiff, and points up and away from your body.

Penis points

● **Penises are usually flaccid, which means soft and hanging down. But sometimes they can be erect, which means hard and pointing upwards.**

● **Flaccid penises can vary quite a lot in size, but erect penises tend to be pretty much the same size.**

● **In spite of what some boys say, girls aren't interested in the size of a boy's penis — it's his personality that counts.**

He's got a great smile...

...and he really makes me laugh.

About erections

When you get an erection, blood rushes into your penis and fills up lots of tiny chambers or spaces inside it. This makes the penis go stiff and hard (a bit like a balloon when it is full of air).

History, history... think about history...

Why do they happen?

The reason a penis becomes erect is so it can be pushed inside a woman's vagina and ejaculate sperm there. When men and women do this it is called sexual intercourse or just "having sex."

Men usually get erections when they are sexually excited. But sometimes they get them just because they are feeling relaxed and happy. Erections are something your body does all by itself, there is not much you can do to control them.

Ups and downs

Before puberty your penis might have become stiff sometimes, but this was not really an erection. During puberty, erections can happen a lot! It's as if your penis has learned a new trick and is practicing for all it's worth, and not only when you are thinking about girls.

You might find yourself getting erections at the weirdest times, often when you least want one — like in the middle of a class at school, or going home on the bus. It can be embarrassing, but the only thing you can do is put your schoolbag, book, or jacket in your lap and try to think about something else while you wait for it to go away.

You might have lots of erections every day, or just every now and then, or hardly have any at all. However it happens for you, it is all perfectly natural and will settle down as you get older.

If you ejaculate, your erection will die down almost right away. If you don't ejaculate it will take longer to fade away. Either way, it doesn't make any difference to your penis or your health.

In your sleep

At first, many boys find that they ejaculate in their sleep at night. This is known as having "wet dreams" and you might wake up to find a sticky patch of semen in your bed. Don't worry. It's just your body putting itself through its paces. Let the semen dry and it will wash out when the sheets are washed.

Check it out

Once puberty kicks in, you start to feel very private about your sex organs. The last thing you want is your mom, big sister, or pretty much anyone for that matter, getting a good look at your penis. That's fine, everyone has a right to their personal privacy — but it does mean that YOU are now responsible for keeping your body in good working order.

Taking a look around

The best way to start taking care of yourself is to get to know your own body, particularly your genitals, or sex organs. That means taking a look at them. Unlike girls, it's not too difficult for you to see your own sex organs, at least from above. But it's a good idea to see them from below as well, and for that you'll need a hand mirror.

Find a private place, such as your bedroom or the bathroom, and then have a good look around. Don't be afraid to handle your genitals, and don't worry if you feel a little silly. Remember, if you know how they look and feel when everything is fine, you'll soon be able to spot it if anything changes.

Cleaning up

The end of your penis is shaped like an old-fashioned soldier's helmet with a hole in the top. This is the glans. It may be covered with a loose sleeve of skin, called the foreskin,

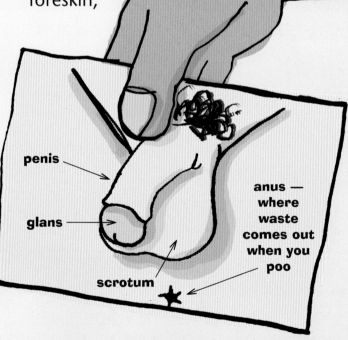

penis

glans

scrotum

anus — where waste comes out when you poo

This is how your penis and scrotum might look from underneath.

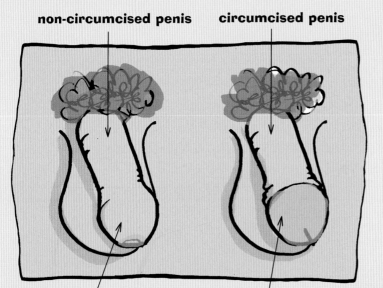

non-circumcised penis   circumcised penis

foreskin covering glans

most of
foreskin
removed

Circumcision

Often boys are circumcised for religious or traditional reasons, usually soon after they are born.

Sometimes boys are circumcised because their family believes that it is cleaner and healthier. However, there is no medical proof that this is true.

which you can slide forward or backward. Not all boys or men have a foreskin. Sometimes it is removed when they are babies, in an operation called circumcision. Foreskins protect the glans. They also produce a creamy paste, called smegma, which helps the skin to slide back and forth.

It is important to keep your penis clean, especially around the glans and foreskin. Wash your genitals at least once a day with soap or body-wash and warm water. If you have a foreskin gently pull it back and wash underneath it to stop too much smegma building up.

Masturbation

Most boys discover at some time or another that touching and rubbing their penis in private feels good. During and after puberty, rubbing your penis will often give you an erection — but not always, especially if you are anxious or in a hurry.

Rubbing your penis like this is called masturbating and it often ends in ejaculation — although, not always. Don't feel bad about masturbating. It will not make you blind, or give you hairy palms! It is a perfectly healthy and normal way to get to …

… know your body!

How do you feel?

By now you could be thinking that puberty sounds like a lot of hassle, and in some ways you are right. It is a time of big changes in your life and changes can be uncomfortable.

Down in the dumps

Suddenly it seems as if nothing is how it used to be, even the way you feel about things. One minute you are just getting on with life as usual, and the next you are down and dismal and fed up with it all.

Sometimes you think your parents and family are great and you love having them around, and other times you wish they would all just go away and leave you alone! Or you wake up one morning and decide that all the clothes you own are completely wrong and you don't have anything to wear — and your hairstyle is horrible.

A balancing act

Some of these sudden shifts and swings in your feelings are caused by those hormones again. There are so many of them in your body that it puts everything out of balance, including your emotions. Not all of your mood changes are caused by hormones, however. As you go through your teens you change from a child to an adult, and your view of yourself and the world begins to alter.

AAARRGH!!

A changing view

The things that you enjoyed when you were younger seem boring and "babyish." You become more aware of the outside world and all the new and exciting things it has to offer. Suddenly there are a lot of different things to do, places to go, and people to discover, and you want to be part of it all … or do you?

Take a break

Growing up is a really busy time, and it is easy to feel swamped by it. These are the times when you find yourself secretly wishing you were "just a kid" again. That's okay. The point about being in-between a child and a grown-up is that it's fine to be a little of both.

Give yourself a break. Relax with a few of your old toys or books. And get plenty of sleep. Your body uses up energy while it's growing, and when you are tired even tiny problems can seem huge.

Finding out about feelings

Some people find it very hard to talk about their feelings, or even to let their real feelings show. They think it makes them look weak or childish.

But if you keep your feelings locked away and don't listen to them, you will never learn to understand them. And that means you won't be able to control them.

Learning about your own feelings can take a long time. It helps to talk to someone about them, especially an older person who you trust.

Sometimes I get so angry with everybody and I don't know why…

Family feuding

As a child you rely on your family to feed you, buy your clothes, keep you healthy, and generally take care of you. Then you become a teenager and you start wanting to do things differently ...

Being independent

You want to make more decisions for yourself about how you live your life: what you wear, what you do, who your friends are and where you go. You probably feel that your parents are old fashioned and out of touch, and you know better than they do about what is right for you. In other words, you want more independence.

But you cannot be completely independent of your family. You still need them to feed and shelter you. And, most of all, you still need their love and support.

Remember that your parents have looked after you all your life so far. It is hard for them to suddenly step back.

Parent worries

At the same time, your parents may find it hard to accept that you are not a child any longer and are able to think for yourself. Or, they may recognize that you are

It's not fair!

growing up and need more space, but worry that you could make the wrong decisions and get into trouble or get behind with your schoolwork. This clash between what you want and what your parents want can lead to arguments and unhappiness for everybody. Parents and teenagers can both feel irritated and hurt by each other. Parents often feel rejected by their children, and teenagers feel that their parents don't understand or trust them.

Keeping in touch

Even if you have a wonderful relationship with your family, the odds are that you will argue about something at some point. It is all part of the growing up process. Although it can be hard sometimes, the best way of sorting things out with your parents is to talk to them — and listen to their worries and their advice, even if you don't always take it.

Make sure they always know what your plans and ideas are. Tell them where you are going and what time you expect to be home. Include

them, rather than shut them out, and be willing to compromise on some of your wants.

Perfect balance

It may take a little time, but if you show them that you can think about others as well as yourself, and that you can balance the needs of your schoolwork and your family with your own desires, they will learn to relax and have confidence in you.

That's okay, honey, I trust you.

Thanks, mom.

Who am I?

It isn't always easy to know what kind of person you are, or who you want to be when you grow up. In fact, some people take their whole lives finding out about themselves. Puberty is the time when you first start asking these kinds of questions, and they can leave you feeling totally confused!

Trying things out

At first, an honest answer might be, "I haven't got a clue!" Most young people try out different styles and ways of behavior just to see how they fit. If you don't feel comfortable then it is fine to try something else.

Listen and learn

But it's also a good idea to be aware of how easily we can be influenced, or changed, by other people. Listening to other people's opinions is a useful way of learning about our world. But we still need to ask ourselves if their opinions work for us.

For example, lots of teenagers are influenced by the way TV celebrities and people in magazines and music videos behave and dress. They think that if they don't look and behave in the same way they will be seen as "losers."

Nope!
Think I'll try this other one.

Trying out different lifestyles can be like trying on clothes. You have to find something that works for you.

TOUGH

HAPPY

Bullying

Wanting to be part of a group can lead to ganging up on someone. Sadly, the more that some people can bully others the better it makes them feel about themselves. This is always wrong. It is never right to make one person suffer just because they are different from you in some way.

If you or someone you know is being bullied you should always tell a responsible adult. It is not telling tales, or being weak, it is simply the right thing to do.

But in spite of their success, many celebrities are deeply unhappy. So instead of trying to copy someone else's lifestyle, it is much more important for each of us to find out what makes US happy.

Fitting in

Friends and other people our own age also influence the way we think and behave. Often this is a good thing. Friends listen to our problems, give us support and advice, and make life much more fun and exciting. But good friends should also care about you. They should not try to force you into doing things that could be harmful or dangerous — to you or to anyone else.

Sometimes you need to have the courage to think for yourself, and if you find that you really don't want to do everything your friends do then you should say so — even if it means being on your own for a while. Being on your own is not a bad thing. It can remind you that one of the best friends you have …

… is yourself!

Relationships

Human beings like to hang out together

and the different ways that we do this make up the different kinds of relationships we have with one another.

When you are a child, relationships are simple. You don't often ask yourself how you feel about your family, friends, and the other people around you, they are just there. Then puberty happens and you begin to look at people differently — and they start looking at you differently, too!

At the center

Your family still loves and cares for you, but now they expect you to be helpful around the house and think about others as well as yourself. Suddenly you realize that you are not the center of your universe anymore, and that other people have needs and wants too, just like you do.

Being responsible

Getting used to this idea can be quite hard at first, and you might feel that it's all very unfair. But look again at pages 50–51. Having more freedom to do the things that you want to do is only one part of being independent. The other part is about being a responsible person.

Thinking ahead

Being responsible means more than just making your own choices. It means thinking about how those choices might hurt or upset someone else — before you act on them! It means respecting other people and their property. And it means saying sorry and doing what you can to put things right when you have messed up — which you are bound to do sometimes, because everybody does.

I'm really sorry, but my kid brother scratched your CD so I bought you a new one.

Taking responsibility for yourself and your actions is not always easy, particularly if it means going without something that you want. But it will help you to build strong relationships based on support and trust — and those are the very best kinds to have.

Stay calm. Dad may be right!

Who's in charge?

Children often scream and shout when they think something is unfair or they can't have what they want. Being a grown-up means trying to take charge of your feelings rather than letting them take charge of you.

So the next time you feel like losing your temper, try to keep calm and think about the other person's point of view first.

Friendships

Relationships with friends are incredibly important, but they are not always as straightforward as they should be. You aren't the only one that is changing — your friends are too!

Making new friends

Sometimes the friends that you've had through childhood become interested in things that don't interest you, and you stop seeing so much of each other. Or, you move to a new or bigger school and you have to start making a new set of friends all over again.

Finding new friends can be tough, particularly in a new school and when puberty makes you feel self-conscious and unsure of yourself. It helps to remember that few kids your age are as cool and confident as they might look. Under the surface, most of them have the same doubts and fears that you do.

I've got great teeth and I'm really good at math!

I've got a nice smile and I'm really good at sports!

Build up your confidence by reminding yourself in the mirror of your good points rather than your bad.

HAPPY BIRTHDAY LUCY

Hi... er... I'm Ben. How long have you known Lucy?

The opposite sex

Another big change that happens during puberty is that you stop seeing the other kids around you as just kids, and start thinking of them as the opposite sex. Girls hang out mainly with girls, and boys with boys. And when the two groups get together they can feel awkward and unsure how to behave to each other.

New feelings

Maybe you get a funny feeling in your stomach when a particular boy or girl talks to you or smiles at you. You may not realize it, but it's those hormones at work again. They not

Shyness

Feeling awkward and shy is a teenage curse, especially at parties. But don't hide away waiting for people to come to you. Take a deep breath and start up a conversation.

Asking someone about themselves is a good way to start. But don't be too pushy. If that person doesn't want to talk to you, try someone else — and keep on trying. The more you do it the easier it is.

only wake up your sex organs and kick them into action, they also wake up your sexual feelings — and that's when you start looking at people in a whole new way.

Finding out about sexual feelings

Discovering that you have sexual feelings for another person doesn't mean you are going to HAVE sex with them. Most people don't start having intercourse until they are in their late teens or older. There's a lot of learning to do first.

Starting out

When you first get interested in someone it might not be anyone your age. It could be a famous pop star, the friend of an older brother or sister, or the guy who works in the local pizza restaurant.

That's the guy from the library, isn't he gorgeous?

It might last for days or months, but while it lasts you are totally wrapped up in that person. You want to know all about them and you daydream about being with them. In other words, you have a crush on them.

Crushes

Crushes are a great way of imagining what a sexual relationship is like, without ACTUALLY having one. You might not believe it at the time, but you aren't really in love with this person, you are just practicing.

Crushes almost never turn into real relationships, and if you have a crush on an older person then it should definitely stay in your imagination.

Any kind of romantic or sexual relationship between a child or young teenager and an older person or an adult is never okay.

What about being gay?

Not everyone has crushes on people of the opposite sex. Girls might daydream about other girls or older women, and boys might daydream about other boys or older men. This does not mean that they will ever have a sexual relationship with someone of the same sex.

Hey, look. Those boys must be gay.

People who have romantic or sexual relationships with people of the same sex are called homosexual, or "gay." Gay women are also known as lesbians. People who have sexual relationships with people of the opposite sex are called heterosexual, or "straight."

Your own sexuality

Finding out the kind of relationships that are right for you takes time. There's no need to rush into a sexual relationship with someone just to prove something to yourself. In the meantime, if you are worried or unsure about it, talk it over with someone you trust. Or talk to a counselor (see page 73).

When two men or two women hug or put their arms around each other it does not necessarily mean that they are gay.

What about dating?

At some point, you are going to find yourself getting interested in a boy or girl that you know. Or maybe he or she is interested in you! The problem is, what do you do next?

Hey... um... do you want to go skating this Saturday?

Dating is when you spend time with a particular person that you feel attracted to, so you can get to know each other better. You might go somewhere special, such as the movies or a restaurant, or you might just meet in the park, or walk home from school together.

Dating rules OK

Most parents have rules about dating, and it's sensible to follow them. Dating before you are old enough to really understand what you are doing is not a good idea.

There's no need to rush. Most kids start dating when they are in their mid-teens or older, and that's absolutely fine. It's usually more fun going out with a group of boys and girls than separating off into pairs of "boyfriends" and "girlfriends."

Boyfriends, girlfriends

In fact, having friends of the opposite sex who really ARE your friends is much better than dating, at least to begin with. It gives you time to get used to being with each other without feeling that you have to have any kind of romantic relationship.

But don't forget that you are all on a different puberty timescale, so if some of your friends seem far more interested in the opposite sex than you are, just remind yourself that it's their hormones.

Friends forever

If one of your friends does start dating, especially if it is your best friend, it is easy to feel left out, or even jealous or hurt. If you can, try not to let your friend know how you feel. Instead, make sure they know that you are still there when they need you, and spend more time with your other friends for a while.

Be patient, at this stage in your lives friendships usually last longer ...

... than dates!

RIGHT WAY

Oh... thanks, but I'm already going out with some friends.

WRONG WAY

What? Go out with you? You must be joking!

Never feel you have to go on a date if you don't want to. It's fine to say no — just do it politely!

Taking care

We have lots of ways of expressing our feelings for each other. We can tell people how we feel, or we might do things for them, or give them presents. Or we might hug them or physically touch them in some way. But there are right and wrong ways of letting people know how we feel about them, and part of growing up is learning to know which is which.

Take your time

Your first date with someone is often nerve-wracking as well as exciting. How are you supposed to behave, for example? Should you hold hands with each other or kiss?

The answer to that is a big "NO" — not if you don't want to. You NEVER have to kiss or hold hands with anyone if you don't want to — ESPECIALLY on a date. And if you do want to, make sure you ask the other person first. Remember, you may not both feel the same way about it!

Don't force yourself

It's fine to want to show someone that you are interested in them, but you should never try to force your feelings

onto someone, or let them force their feelings onto you — no matter how much you might like them, or want them to like you. One of the hardest lessons we have to learn is accepting the fact that not everyone we like is going to feel the same way about us.

Showing off

Sometimes people try to impress someone they like by teasing them or making comments about the way that person looks or behaves. People show off like this when they are unsure of themselves and haven't yet learned that, although teasing will get them noticed, it won't make them liked!

Paying attention

It can be flattering when someone pays special attention to you. But if that person says things about you that you don't like, or wants to flirt or touch you in ways that you don't want, then it is absolutely okay to tell them to stop, no matter who they are. If they don't stop, tell a parent, teacher, or another adult you trust, even if you feel embarrassed. Don't ever think that it is your fault — IT ISN'T!

I hate it when Max teases me. He thinks he's so smart, but he's just a show-off!

Staying safe

Unfortunately, there are always a few people in the world who are unkind or even dangerous to others, and it is not always easy to know who they are. As you get older and go out more, with friends or on your own, you need to know how to keep yourself safe.

GOLDEN RULES FOR GOING OUT

● **Never travel on your own after dark or in badly lit or remote places. Always stay with your friends.**

● **Make sure your parents or other adults always know where you are going and when you expect to be back.**

● **Remember that drugs and alcohol stop you from thinking clearly, and don't put yourself at risk from others who have been taking them.**

● **Never get into a car or truck with anyone you and your parents do not know.**

● **Do not talk to strangers who approach you, even if they are older kids or they know your name. And do not take food, drinks, or anything from them.**

● **If someone is bothering you and they won't leave you alone, shout or scream until they do — no matter who it is!**

● **If you need help, go to a busy shop or restaurant where there are lots of adults and ask for help there.**

On the Internet

You don't have to go out to be at risk. If you use the Internet and visit chat rooms you might make contact with people who lie about their age and who they are. Never give anyone you talk to on the Internet your phone number or address, and never arrange to meet them.

Mobile mobsters

Some people think it's cool or funny to send nasty messages or pictures to other people's cell phones. This is a type of bullying. If you ever get a message like this, even if you think it is meant as a joke, you must show your parents or another responsible adult.

Not worth the risk

The best way to be safe is to be sensible. Don't take risks just because someone else says it will be fun — even if that someone is a friend. This is especially true when it comes to alcohol and drugs. Lots of kids start drinking or taking drugs because their friends persuade them to. Even aside from the fact that it is against the law, these things are extremely dangerous.

The biggest danger is that you never know what affect they will have on you. They change the way you think and behave, making it much more likely that you will do something you would not normally do. And, because they are poisons, they can do serious damage to your health.

Understanding abuse

If anyone ever tries to touch you in ways that make you frightened or uncomfortable, or talk to you in a sexual way, or show you pictures of people having sex, they are sexually abusing you and they are doing something WRONG!

How can I possibly tell anyone? Who would believe me?

Don't keep it secret

Any form of abuse is horrible and extremely frightening. But no matter what the abuser or anyone else may tell you, it is NEVER your fault.

Sexual abuse is a difficult thing to understand, and it can be very hard to talk about. It is especially difficult if the person abusing you is not a stranger but someone you know, such as one of your parent's friends or a neighbor. He or she might even be a member of your own family. But whoever it is, all adults know that abuse is wrong, and it should never be kept a secret.

If bad things happen

If you are bullied, or threatened or abused in any way, you must tell someone — as soon as possible. The best people to tell are your parents or guardians. But if you can't talk to them about it, then find another responsible adult, such as a teacher, or one of your friends' parents.

Keep trying, even if it is hard to find someone to listen to you. There are organizations and helplines that you can call who will do their best to help you and give you advice. Some of them are listed on page 75.

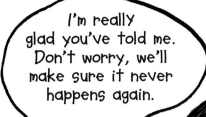

I'm really glad you've told me. Don't worry, we'll make sure it never happens again.

What's okay and what's not

It is never okay for someone to touch you in a way that you don't want to be touched. But remember that not everyone who wants to give you a hug or a kiss on the cheek is a sexual abuser. In fact, very few people in the world are.

The kind of hugging and kissing that goes on in most families and between friends is a natural and necessary part of life.

Are You hurt? Can I help?

Whatever you do, don't try to shut the problem away and ignore it. If you do that, the memory of it, and the bad feelings it brings you, will be with you forever. The best way to deal with any kind of problem, but particularly one as hurtful and dangerous as abuse, is …

… talk about it!

Also, if you have an accident or hurt yourself and someone tries to help you, this does not mean that person is an abuser, either.

Abusers are people who threaten or frighten you, or want you to do things in private where no one else can see what they are doing!

Be healthy, be happy

You own your body. It belongs to you

and no one else has the right to make you do anything with it that you don't want to do. BUT the fact that you own it means that your body depends on YOU to take care of it.

Making choices

As you grow up and become more independent, you begin making more choices for yourself. Some of these choices are about the type of food you eat, how active you are, or how much sleep you get. These kinds of choices are important, because they can make the difference between a healthy body and an unhealthy body.

I'm starving, let's go get a coke and a doughnut.

I'd rather have a fruit smoothie!

Food for life

Food is vital, without it you would run out of energy and die. But in order to make the right kind of food choices it's helpful to know what different types of foods do for you.

Energy foods

Most foods can be divided into five main groups. A lot of the energy your body uses comes from the grains group. This group includes bread, pasta, rice, other cereals, and potatoes. Foods that have "whole grains" in them, such as whole wheat bread, and brown rice, are especially good for you because they also have lots of fiber. Your body needs fiber to

> Sugary foods taste great, but you need to use up the energy they give you.

types are better for us than others. Friendly fats are found in plant oils, such as olive and peanut oil, and in fish. Fats are also in meat and butter, and in margarines and the pre-cooked foods you buy in shops, such as muffins, chips, and fries. Too much of these fats are harmful to your heart.

Sugars are found in sweet foods, such as cakes, cookies, ice cream, and soda. Sugar is a source of energy, but if you don't use that energy, it is stored as body fat.

help digest or break down other food. Fiber also fills you up and isn't stored by your body as fat!

Making and mending
Your body needs regular amounts of something called protein, to help it build new cells and mend damaged ones. The protein group includes meat, fish, eggs, beans, and nuts.

Fats and sugars
Small amounts of fats are vital for our brain, nerves, and skin. But some

Full of fiber
Vegetables and fruits are a fantastic source of fiber, and they are full of vitamins and minerals. We need a lot of vitamins and minerals to help our bodies grow and work properly.

Bones and teeth
Milk and other dairy foods, such as cheese and yogurt, contain fats, protein, and some vitamins. But they also contain lots of the mineral calcium, which our bodies need to build strong bones and teeth.

Keeping your balance

Making healthy food choices and having a well balanced diet is all about eating a variety of different foods from each food group, and eating the right amount.

GRAINS — breads and other cereals (especially whole grain), and potatoes. About 3–5 different portions a day, but don't add too much extra fat or sugar to them.

FRUIT AND VEGETABLES — eat lots of these every day. At least 5 different portions a day is excellent.

PROTEIN FOODS — meat, fish, eggs, beans and nuts. Eat 2–3 different portions a day.

DAIRY FOODS — milk, cheese, and yogurt. Eat 2–3 different portions a day, preferably low-fat.

FATS AND SUGARS — cooking oils, spreads, fried food, chocolate, cookies, cakes, biscuits, etc. Eat small amounts of fats and as little sugar as possible.

Water, water, water

We don't only need to give our body food, it needs plenty of liquids as well, especially water.

Try to drink 6–8 glasses a day, but avoid too many sugary drinks and fruit juices.

The food on your plate

One way of thinking about the food you eat every day is to imagine it as a plate with different colored sections like the one shown here. Each section stands for one of the five food groups.

The size of each section shows you roughly how much of your food should come from each group. So you can see that you should try to eat more fruits, vegetables, grains and potatoes each day, then protein and dairy foods, and only eat a small amount of fatty or sugary foods.

How much is enough?

Eating a mixture of foods from each food group will give your body the

Eating disorders

We need to think about the food that we eat, but some people worry so much about food that it makes them ill.

This kind of illness is called an eating disorder. Sometimes people are so afraid of being overweight they almost stop eating and become dangerously thin. Or they secretly eat huge amounts of food and then make themselves sick to get rid of it. Or they cannot stop themselves from eating far more food than they need and become very overweight.

Absolutely anyone can have an eating disorder. It often makes people feel guilty and ashamed, but it is important to get help as soon as possible. If you think that you or anyone you know may have an eating disorder, talk about it with an adult you trust.

goodness it needs, but the amount of food you eat matters, too. If you do not eat enough protein, grains or dairy foods, for example, you will be lacking in energy and may not grow properly. If you eat too many fried, fatty, or sugary foods you will become unhealthy and overweight — especially if you don't exercise.

Get up and go

As well as eating the right kinds of food, the best thing you can do for your body is give it plenty of exercise.

Muscle and bones

Exercise strengthens your bones and muscles and keeps them healthy. It also gives your body shape. Without it, your muscles get weak and flabby, and your body becomes stiff so you cannot move and bend easily.

The heart of the matter

Your heart is a muscle and it needs to be exercised, just like your other muscles. When you exercise you strengthen your heart so that it pumps your blood more easily and quickly around your body. You also breathe more deeply so you get more oxygen into your body. This is good for your whole system. It gives you energy, wakes up your brain, and makes you happy!

The happy hormone

This may sound like something your parents dreamed up to get you away from the TV, but it is true. Exercise releases a hormone in your brain that changes your mood and helps you to feel better about yourself.

The more energy you use the better you feel.

It doesn't matter what exercise you do as long as you do it regularly — at least an hour a day is good.

Along the way

At the beginning of this book I said that growing up was an adventure — and it is! It's full of surprises and challenges. Sometimes it feels like hard work, and other times it's exciting and you will be on top of the world. But whatever happens, always remember that you don't have to do it all alone.

Getting help

Never think that you can't ask for help, no matter how embarrassed, stupid, bad, or frightened you feel. Most adults understand that growing up can be a difficult time and, as long as you explain the problem, they will help you if they can.

Keep trying

If the first person you try can't or won't help, try again until you find someone who will. As well as your own family, there are your friends' families, your teachers, religious advisor, school nurse, or the nurse or doctor at your family practice. People are often nervous about going to see a nurse or a doctor. Or they think their problem isn't important enough. But you should never ignore a health problem, no matter how small or embarrassing it may seem to you.

Hi. Um... I need some advice, can you help me?

Counseling centers

There are also helplines and counseling centers of all kinds that you can contact. A few are listed on page 75, but your local library should have a list of others, too. Above all, don't suffer in silence. No problem is so big that it can't be solved in some way.

Be healthy, be happy 73

Your best friend

The other important thing to remember is that your body is your best friend — even if it can sometimes seem like your worst enemy! Love it, care for it, and treat it with respect.

BE GOOD TO YOURSELF

- Keep your body clean and wash your hair regularly.

- Take care of your adult teeth. Brush them at least twice a day and go to the dentist every six months.

- Don't poison your body with alcohol, drugs, or cigarettes.

- Think about the food you eat and make healthy choices.

- Drink lots of water every day and get plenty of exercise.

- Make sure you get enough sleep. Ten hours a night is good.

- Respect yourself and others.

Be proud

Be proud of your body. No matter what size, shape or sex you are, it really is the most miraculous thing you will ever own. And, most of all ...

... enjoy the adventure!

Finding out more

Help and advice

These organizations will all give you personal advice and information.

* CHILD PROTECTIVE SERVICES: Governmental agency in many states in the United States that responds to child abuse and neglect.

* NATIONAL YOUTH CRISIS HOTLINE: 1-800-442-HOPE—responds to youth crisis.

* NATIONAL ASSOCIATION OF ANOREXIA NERVOSA AND ASSOCIATED DISORDERS: (847) 831-3428
www.anad.org

* COVENANT HOUSE HOTLINE: 1-800-999-9999—Crisis hotline for youth, teens, and families.
www. covenanthouse.org

* NATIONAL SUICIDE PREVENTION LIFELINE: 1-800-273-TALK(8255)—provides immediate assistance to individuals in suicidal crisis.

* GIRLS AND BOYS TOWN NATIONAL HOTLINE: 1-800-448-3000
www.girlsandboystown.org/hotline

Information websites

These websites are all run specifically for young people.

www.kidshealth.org — masses of information on puberty, health, feelings, and problems, plus animations, quizzes, and games. Run by the Nemours Foundation, USA.

www.lifebytes.gov.uk — fun facts and information for 11–14 year olds on health, alcohol, drugs, eating, safety and sex. Run by the Health Education Authority, UK.

www.thehormonefactory.com — fun information for 10-12 year olds on puberty. Run by the Australian Research Centre in Sex, Health & Society.

Useful words

When you see words in small capitals, LIKE THIS, it means they have a separate entry of their own.

Abuse
When someone frightens or hurts you in a physical, sexual, or emotional way.

Anti-perspirant
A chemical that blocks the pores (tiny holes) in your skin to stop sweat from getting out.

Anus
The hole in your bottom through which you poo.

Bacteria
Tiny living things that live in us and all around us. Some bacteria are harmful and can make us ill, but many keep us healthy.

Cells
All living things are made of cells. Some BACTERIA are made of just one cell. We are made of millions of cells. Most cells are too small to see. The largest single cell is a bird's egg.

Clitoris
A small bundle of nerves at the front of the VULVA. Part of a woman's SEX ORGANS.

Deodorant
A chemical that kills some of the BACTERIA on your skin that makes sweat smell.

Egg cell
The female sex CELL. When it is FERTILIZED by a SPERM CELL it grows into a baby.

Ejaculating
When SEMEN rushes out of the end of the PENIS, usually during an ERECTION.

Epididymis
A thin tube coiled around each TESTICLE, which stores SPERM CELLS.

Erection
When blood rushes into a PENIS, making it swollen and stiff so it can be put into a woman's VAGINA.

Fertilized
When a SPERM CELL enters an EGG CELL and the two cells join together.

Foreskin
A double fold of skin that covers and protects the end of the PENIS.

Growth spurt
A time during PUBERTY when your body grows especially quickly.

Hormones
Chemicals made in the parts of your body called glands and carried around in your blood. Hormones act on other parts of your body, making them stop or start doing things.

Intercourse
When a man puts his PENIS inside a woman's VAGINA. Also known as "having sex."

Menstrual cycle
The number of days from the first day of one PERIOD, to the first day of the next.

Ovaries

The parts of a woman's SEX ORGANS where her EGG CELLS are stored.

Penis

The part of a man's SEX ORGANS that delivers SEMEN into a woman's VAGINA. Also used to let out urine (pee) from the body.

Periods

The number of days each month when blood and other liquids leave a woman's UTERUS, carrying an unfertilized EGG with it.

Puberty

The period of time during which your body changes from a child to an adult and you become able to produce children.

Pubic hair

The hair that grows around your PENIS or VULVA.

Scrotum

The loose sack of skin that hangs behind the PENIS and contains the TESTICLES.

Semen

The white, milky mixture of SPERM CELLS and fluid that comes out of the PENIS during EJACULATION.

Sex organs

All the parts of the body, both on the inside and on the outside, that are involved in making babies.

Sperm cell

The male sex CELL. When a sperm cell FERTILIZES an EGG CELL it grows into a baby.

Sweat glands

Tiny sacks inside your skin that produce sweat.

Testicles

The parts of a man's SEX ORGANS that make and store SPERM CELLS.

Umbilical cord

A bendy, twisted tube that allows food and oxygen to pass from the mother to a baby while it is developing in the UTERUS.

Uterus

Part of a woman's SEX ORGANS in which a FERTILIZED EGG CELL grows into a baby.

Vagina

Part of a woman's SEX ORGANS. SPERM CELLS pass from a man's PENIS into the VAGINA in order to reach an EGG CELL. Unfertilized egg cells leave a woman's body through the vagina, and babies also travel through it to be born.

Vaginal discharge

A clear or creamy liquid coming from the vagina. If a discharge is discolored or smelly it might mean that you have an infection.

Vas deferens

A tube that carries SPERM CELLS from the EPIDIDYMIS to the PENIS.

Vulva

A woman's outer SEX ORGANS, including the CLITORIS and the opening to the VAGINA.

Wet dreams

EJACULATING in your sleep during PUBERTY.

Index

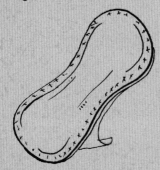